FROM A CHILD'S HEART

poems by Nikki Grimes
pictures by Brenda Joysmith

Printed in U.S.A./First Edition 10 9 8 7 6 5 4
Library of Congress Catalog Number 93-79000
ISBN: 0-940975-44-0 (hardcover) 0-940975-43-2 (paper)

JUST US BOOKS
East Orange, New Jersey

A Personal Note

God is never far away. We only think He is. Sometimes it takes a child to remind us of that, which, when you think about it, makes perfect sense: Children are closer to the source. They seem to know that God's nearby, that we can talk to Him anytime, anywhere, in any language—straight from the heart.

Like the children in this book, when I was a child, I talked to God about my hopes, my fears, my longings, and all the ordinary, everyday concerns that touched my life. I still do. It's awesome to know that the God of the Universe is listening, that He cares, that He understands me, even when no one else does. I needed to know that when I was growing up. I think all children do, whether five years old or fifty. That's the reason I've decided to share the prayers of my childhood with you. Thanks for reading them. And thank You, God, for listening!

CONTENTS

From A Child's Heart

A CREDIT

Heavenly Father, please help me to be
the best me I know how.
I'm little now but someday
I'm sure I could do somethin' grand.
I could buy a zillion acres of land,
grow enough food to feed everyone.
I could be the smartest person on this whole earth
or somebody *r e a l* famous who is worth
talkin' about. Maybe a preacher
like Martin Luther King, Jr. Mama says
I can be anything if I only believe.
And I believe I want to be
a credit to the human race.

GOOD MORNING, LORD

Good morning, Lord.
Don't laugh.
I know You saw me peeking at the ground and sky
to make sure that the sky was blue, the street was dry
so Mom and me could go out to the park.
Yesterday fat rain clouds made the morning dark.
(No offense, Lord, but I hate it when it rains on the weekend.)
Weekends are the only time I have Mom to myself,
in the afternoons, at least.
Wish she had more time to play
but I'm glad she has some time today.
Thank You for the sun.

FRIENDSHIP

Since we moved here, God,
You're the only friend I've got
which is okay, I guess—
or maybe not. I mean,
I sure would like to have a buddy my own size.
I bet You know that, though,
since Mama says You're wise.
Could You give me a new friend?
Someone with a basketball?
You and me will still be friends and all,
But right now,
I need somebody who'll invite me out to play.
Is that okay?

NUMBER ONE

Dear God, I want to solo
You know: to dance.
But I don't want to get the chance
just 'cause the color of my skin keeps me from fitting in
with everyone else in class.
Let them choose me 'cause I'm good,
'cause I can to do something that no one else could.
Give me the hardest step, I'll learn it.
Make me number one, Lord. I'll earn it
long as You're by my side.

DADDY'S HAT

My daddy's hard hat is way too big for me.
I walked around in it today
but I could hardly see
to build my pretend house
or finish off the bridge like daddy taught me to.
He had nothing else to do
'cause they laid him off again.

But God, if You're his friend,
please give my daddy work
and I'll find something else to play.
He can have his old hard hat,
Okay?

SIDEYARD

The wind sang and sighed like an old woman spookin'
the dogwood trees back of grandma's house last night.
My little brother said it was an awful fright,
but me, I loved it.
I never heard the wind sing or sigh before,
not where we live in the city.
And the garden is so pretty!
I never saw so many flowers, Lord.
You see the way those roses hug the porch and climb the stair?
Just like they love this timber house and hardly care
if everybody knows.
But those roses don't love this house half as much as me.
Bless grandma, Lord, for inviting us to stay
And by the way,
ask her if we can stay again next year.

BOOK REPORT

Another book report is due
and there's a test in math next week.
I need a miracle from You, if You don't mind.
Say what?
I should study for the test?
Read the book? Do my best?
Then You'll help me remember what I've learned?
Well, that sounds fair,
long as I know that You'll be there.

BIG SISTER SAYS

Sis always says
"If you're gonna do something, do it right."
So when I do my homework every night,
I draw my letters straight and neat in my notebook.
I know the teacher may not take the time to look,
but Sis says do it anyway, even if nobody else can see—
except You, Lord, and me.

NIGHT FIGHT

There they go again, Lord.
My mom and daddy screamin'
and I wonder if they're meanin'
half of what they say.

God, please make them stop.
Is there something I can do?
Maybe try real hard to listen,
do what my mom tells me to.
Maybe stay out of the way,
try to be one less problem,
and not one more.

FROM A CHILD'S HEART

I've been here all afternoon.
Mama's coming for me soon.
I hope she takes her time.

I love being with my friend,
not having to speak,
rubbing a blade of grass to make it squeak,
and lying in the sun.

This summer fun is going by too fast.
God, would You please make it last?
Or, if You'd rather not,
please make each day that's left
feel like forever.

ONE MORE YEAR

Lord,
Please give my Grandma one more year. Just one.
I know she's been around a while,
but You don't need her half as bad as me.
You see, she's been my mom and dad as far back as memory goes
and she knows the ins and outs of being free inside.
When she got sick last night, I cried.
Don't know what I'd do without her.
I guess I'd make it if I tried,
but I can wait.
Can't You?

SPACE

We need space, God.
Just a little.
We're so many, seems there isn't any room to grow.
I don't know.
Don't mind being close sometimes,
but three in a bed gets kinda tight,
and I always end up having to fight
for cover.

My mother says one day we'll move to a bigger place,
but it sure would help if we had more space right now—
just a little.
And Lord, while You're at it,
how about an extra bed?

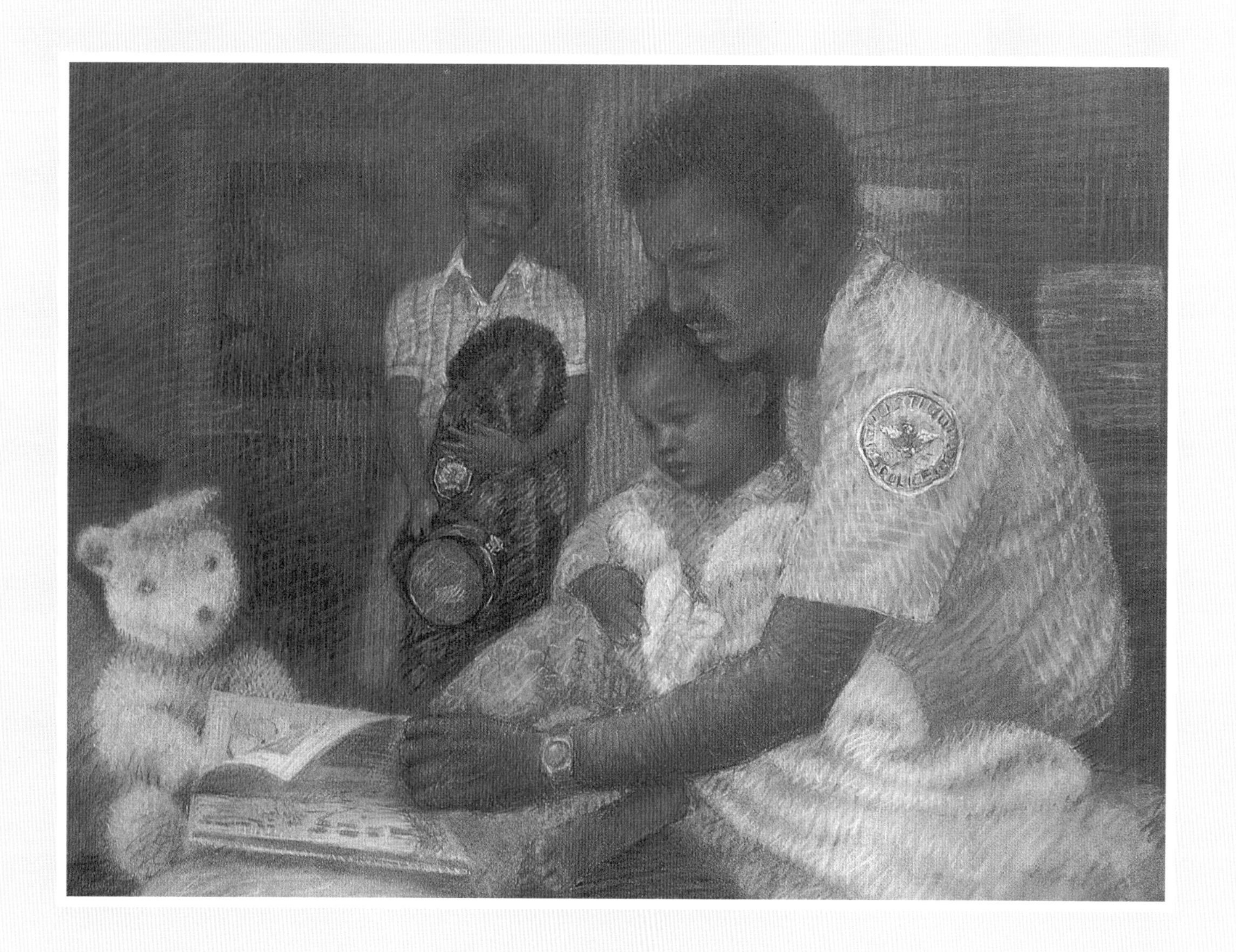

GOOD NIGHT, LORD

Mom says that You love me, Lord, just as I am
But could that really be true?
This morning I wanted to play basketball
but Big Boy said I wouldn't do.
He said, "You're too short and you're too young besides."
I'm always too something in somebody's eyes:
Too short or too thin, too weak or too strong.
Lord, I get the feeling that I'm made all wrong.
Then You whip up a perfectly starry night,
And I know if You made me, I must be all right.
So thanks, Lord, for making me.
Oh, yeah! There's one more thing—
Good night!

ACKNOWLEDGMENTS & PICTURE CREDITS

The poems *Space* and *Book Report* were first published in *Bubbles: Poetry for Fun and Meaning*, Theodore E. Wade, Jr., Ed. Gazelle Publications, 1987.

The pastel drawings reproduced in *From a Child's Heart* are property of Brenda Joysmith or are found in various private collections. Original drawings are pastel on paper. Their titles and the pages on which they appear are listed below.

front cover, page ii, and page 21	Open Gate, © 1985
facing page 1	Paper Boys, © 1985
page 2	Memories of Waiting, © 1989
page 5	Older Boys, © 1985
page 6	Barefoot Dreams, © 1984
page 9	Part of Growing, © 1992
page 10	Sideyard, © 1992
page 12	Reading From All Sides, © 1988
page 15	Day Care, © 1990
page 17	Contemplation V, © 1985
page 18	Princess to Duchess, © 1990
page 20	Fellowship, © 1990
page 22	Doll Play, © 1988
page 24	Ritual of Good Night, © 1991

photo of Nikki Grimes, courtesy Joelle Petit Adkins, © 1993.
photo of Brenda Joysmith, courtesy Joysmith Studio.

NIKKI GRIMES

Nikki Grimes is a poet, journalist and author whose books for children and young adults include: *Growin'*, a novel; *Something On My Mind*, an ALA Notable Book of verse, and *Malcolm X: A Force for Change*, a biography. An accomplished writer of adult poetry, her children's verse has appeared on the pages of *Cricket Magazine*, and in anthologies such as *Bubbles: Poetry for Fun and Meaning*, *A World of Poetry*, and *Pass It On: African-American Poetry for Children*. She has conducted readings and lectures at colleges and universities across the country, as well as in Europe and in Africa.

Formerly a writer/editor for the Walt Disney Company, Ms. Grimes now divides her time between writing books and designing handknitted art-to-wear garments and accessories. She lives in California.

BRENDA JOYSMITH

Born and raised in Memphis, Tennessee, Brenda Joysmith began her career as a child—creating portraits of her friends. Her talent eventually led her to study at the University of Chicago, where she received her Bachelor's degree in Fine Arts.

Ms. Joysmith's work has been featured in galleries from Philadelphia to San Francisco, on the hit sitcom *The Cosby Show*, in the films, *Lethal Weapon II and III*, and in the children's book *Shake it to the One That You Love the Best*.

The growing recognition for African-American art has created a specific demand for Ms. Joysmith's work. She says her pastels are "a deliberate reach for feelings, memory, and passion." *From a Child's Heart* is her first children's book illustrated exclusively with her own art work. She presently owns and operates the Joysmith Studio in Emeryville, California.